HOCKEY

Robb Johnstone

Weigl Publishers Inc.

Published by Weigl Publishers Inc.
123 South Broad Street, Box 227
Mankato, MN 56002
USA
Copyright © 2001 Weigl Publishers Inc.

Library of Congress Cataloging-in-Publication Data available upon request from the publisher.
Fax: (507) 388-2746 for the attention of the Publishing Records Department.
ISBN 1-930954-15-8

Printed in the United States of America
3 4 5 6 7 8 9 05 04 03

Project Coordinator
Rennay Craats
Layout and Design
Warren Clark
Copy Editor
Heather Kissock

Photograph credits
Cover: Freestyle Photography (André Ringuette); Title: Freestyle Photography (Phillip MacCullum); Contents: R&G Sports Photography (Roy McLean); Canada's Sports Hall of Fame: pages 4, 16; Corel Corporation: page 20B; EyeWire: page 21T; Freestyle Photography: pages10B (André Ringuette),15B (Phillip MacCullum),18L (André Ringuette); Frozen Motion Photography: pages 5B (Bernie Steenbergen),8 (Bernie Steenbergen),11T (Bernie Steenbergen),13T (Bernie Steenbergen); Globe Photos, Inc: page 15T (Kenneth Kaminsky); Hockey Hall of Fame: pages 17,17B (Dave Sandford), 18R,19; Monique de St. Croix: pages 6, 7T, 7M,10T, 11B,12T, 22; Photodisc: page 20T; Reuters/Archive Photos: page 7B (Peter Jones); R & G Sports Photography: pages 5T (Roy McLean), 12B (Roy McLean),13B (Roy McLean) 14R (Roy McLean); Visuals Unlimited: pages14L (Arthur Hill), 21B (Cheyenne Rouse), 23 (Bill Banaszewski).

Contents

What is Hockey?

People disagree on who invented hockey and where it started. Some argue that Native Americans first played a similar game in Canada. However, the person most often credited with inventing hockey is James Creighton. He took part in the first organized hockey game in 1875. A Canadian university student, W.F. Robertson, established the first set of rules.

At first, people played hockey on frozen lakes and rivers. It was only played in cold countries such as Canada. Today, people can play hockey anywhere because of indoor ice rinks.

Hockey players in the early 1900s wore very little padding and protective gear.

There are two teams in a hockey game. Each team tries to put a hard rubber puck into the other team's net. This is called scoring a **goal**. When time runs out, the game is over. The team that scores the most goals wins.

Scoring a goal is a great accomplishment. Even though one player scores the goal, the entire team helps to move the puck toward the net.

Planning is needed to win hockey games.

CHECK IT OUT

To brush up on your hockey knowledge, surf over to
www.hockeyphreak.com

Getting Ready to Play

A long time ago, a hockey player only needed a sheet of ice, a pair of skates, a stick, and a puck. Some people still play hockey this way. It is called "shinny." This is a good name because you can get many bruises on your shins if you do not wear equipment.

A hockey jersey is often large. It has to fit elbow and shoulder pads underneath it.

Hockey pants are like long shorts. Players wear long wool socks or long underwear under the pants. Shin pads are worn under their socks.

Players wear thick gloves. They protect the player's hands and keep them warm. Goalies use gloves like baseball mitts to help them block shots.

Players glide on the ice on skates. Skates have sharp blades on the bottoms. The boots are made of leather or light plastic.

Players use sticks to control the puck. Many people wrap tape around the **blade**, or bottom, of the stick. This helps them handle the puck better. Goalies use different sticks than do other players. Their sticks are wider at the bottom to help them block shots better.

Pucks are small disks made of rubber. Players pass the puck to each other and try to put it in the other team's net. In professional hockey, pucks are frozen before being used. This stops them from bouncing too much on the ice.

Hockey sticks are usually made out of wood. Sometimes they are made from graphite, which is lighter.

Goaltenders use blockers to stop shots. Blockers are pads worn on the goalie's stick hand. They use them to knock the puck away from the net.

The Rink

A hockey rink is a big sheet of ice with a net at each end. High boards surround the ice. There are lines and circles on the ice that are important to the rules of the game.

There is a thick red line in the middle of the ice and two thin red lines near the ends. Two blue lines are painted between the red lines.

The circles on the ice show where the officials drop the puck to start play. When the official drops the puck, it is called a **face-off** because a player from one team faces a player from the other team. They both try to knock the puck to their teammates. As a result, the circles are called face-off circles.

Winning the face-off takes skill and speed. Players have to touch the puck before the other team.

he **boards** around the rink are designed to keep the puck and players inside. There is usually glass or wire **mesh** that sits on top of the boards. This keeps the puck from flying out and hitting people in the stands.

There are two places for players on each team to sit, called benches. There are special gates at the benches that allow players to go onto the ice. There are also two **penalty** boxes where players go when they break the rules.

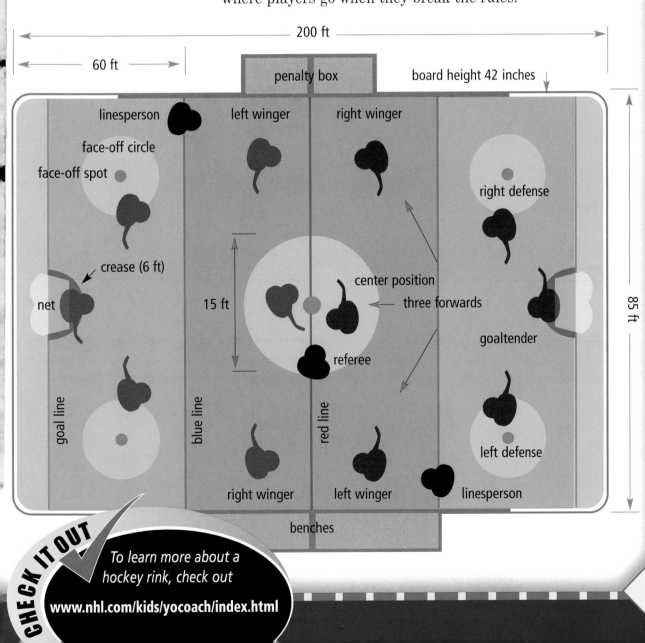

200 ft

60 ft

penalty box

board height 42 inches

linesperson

left winger

right winger

face-off circle

face-off spot

right defense

crease (6 ft)

net

15 ft

center position

three forwards

goaltender

referee

goal line

blue line

red line

left defense

right winger

left winger

linesperson

benches

85 ft

CHECK IT OUT

To learn more about a hockey rink, check out

www.nhl.com/kids/yocoach/index.html

Following the Rules

Players have to follow the rules. They cannot use their sticks to trip or hit other players. They also cannot hold another player back using their hands or sticks. To make sure everyone will be safe, players must keep their sticks below the shoulders. If they do not, they can be called for **high-sticking**.

Players cannot stand by their opponent's net and wait for the puck. If they did, they would be called **offside**. Offside is when a player moves across the other team's blue line before the puck does. Also, players cannot pass the puck across the blue and center lines. This is an offside pass.

Icing is when a player shoots the puck from his or her end of the rink. It crosses the goal line on the other end without anyone touching it. The puck is then brought back to where it was shot from.

Most players like to shoot the puck. Passing the puck to a teammate is just as important.

Hockey can be a very rough game. This is why players wear protective padding and a helmet.

These rules are designed to make sure the game is played fairly and to keep players from being hurt. During the game, a referee watches out for players who break the rules.

The referee uses his hands to signal a penalty and to direct the hockey game.

If a player breaks a rule, the referee blows a whistle and stops the game. Sometimes a player gets sent to the penalty box for breaking a rule. That player's team must play with one fewer player. This gives the other team an advantage, so players are encouraged to always follow the rules. In professional hockey, the referee is joined by two linespeople, who help **enforce** the rules.

Players must wait until their time in the penalty box is finished before re-joining the game.

Positions

There are three positions in hockey: goaltender, defender, and forward. Each team puts one goalie, two defenders, and three forwards on the ice at one time.

Goalies stay in front of the net and keep their opponents from scoring. They wear special equipment to protect them from shots. It takes a lot of bravery to be a goaltender. A puck shot from a stick can travel at more than 100 miles per hour! Goalies usually stay on the ice for the entire game. Other players play in **shifts**.

The goalie is the last line of defense.

Sometimes, players have to use their muscles to keep control of the puck.

CHECK IT OUT

Find out more about the players in these positions at

www.espn.go.com/nhl

The defender's job is similar to the goalie's. They both try to keep other players from scoring. For this reason, defenders usually stay close to their net. Because defenders can go anywhere on the ice, they can also score goals.

A forward's job is to score goals. There is a center forward, a right wing, and a left wing. They all try to break through the other team's defense and take shots on the net.

Forwards use their skating speed to move the puck toward the net.

Making it Big

Early on, players practise skating and decide which position they want to play. As they get older, they get better at hockey and move up from one level to the next— from Mite to Squirt to PeeWee to Bantam.

Players who continue to play into their teens may play on Junior teams. They may also choose to play on college or university teams. These leagues attract attention from professional teams. There are also leagues, including the American Hockey League (AHL) and the International Hockey League (IHL), that act as farm teams for the National Hockey League (NHL).

National teams represent their home countries in international competition.

Practise is important at any age.

Every year, the professional teams get together to choose the young players they want. This is called a **draft**. Each team takes turns picking players until all available players have been chosen. It is a big thrill for players who are chosen first overall. That usually means they are headed for success in the NHL.

Every player in the NHL wants to win the Stanley Cup. The Stanley Cup is the oldest award for professional athletes in North America. It was first given out in 1894. This award is given to the top team at the end of the championship play-offs.

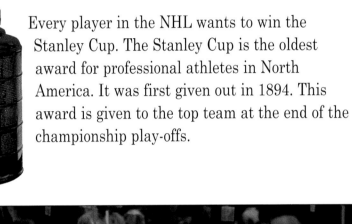

Winning the Stanley Cup is one of the greatest achievements in a player's career.

NHL teams work hard all season to try to reach the play-offs.

CHECK IT OUT

Follow your favorite teams and players, past and present, at
www.hhof.com

15

Superstars of the Sport

Hockey has many past heroes. Many of these heroes inspired today's professionals to play the game.

#9 MAURICE (ROCKET) RICHARD

POSITION:
Right Wing
TEAM:
Montreal Canadiens
SIGNED TO THE NHL:
1942

Career Facts:

- Maurice was known as "The Rocket."
- During his career, Maurice won the Stanley Cup with the Canadiens eight times.
- Maurice was one of the game's greatest goal scorers. At the end of his career, he had scored 544 goals. This was a record at the time.
- Maurice was the first player to score fifty goals in one season. At this time, teams only played fifty games in each season.

#9 GORDIE HOWE

POSITION:
Right Wing
TEAM:
Detroit Red Wings
SIGNED TO THE NHL:
1946

Career Facts:

- Gordie's career lasted from when he was a teenager until he was in his fifties.
- Gordie was known as "Mr. Hockey."
- Gordie's points record of 1,850 lasted until 1989. It was broken by Wayne Gretzky, who was Gordie's biggest fan!
- Gordie stayed in hockey for so long, he got to play on the same team as his two sons.
- In his career, Gordie played 2,421 games and scored 1,071 goals with 1,518 assists. This gave him a professional total of 2,589 points.

#4 BOBBY ORR

POSITION:
Defender
TEAMS:
Boston Bruins,
Chicago Blackhawks
SIGNED TO THE NHL:
1966

Career Facts:

- Bobby changed how people thought of defense players. He was a powerful defender, but he could score goals, too.
- Bobby was the first defender to score more than forty goals in a season.
- Bobby was the first defender to score one hundred points and to win the overall scoring title.
- Bobby was the first hockey player in the world to earn $1 million.

#99 WAYNE GRETZKY

POSITION:
Center
TEAMS:
Edmonton Oilers, L.A.
Kings, St. Louis Blues,
New York Rangers
SIGNED TO THE NHL:
1979

Career Facts:

- In 1989, Wayne broke Gordie Howe's points record. Wayne ended his career with 2,856 points.
- Wayne was a member of the Edmonton Oilers in the 1980s when the team dominated the game.
- Wayne holds sixty-one NHL records.
- In the 1982-1983 **season**, Wayne scored an incredible ninety-two goals!
- Wayne made Los Angeles hockey fans excited about hockey when he was traded to the L.A. Kings in 1988.

CHECK IT OUT

Find out more about sports in an online magazine for kids at

www.sikids.com

Superstars of Today

The hockey stars of today have fans cheering in the stands.

#68 JAROMIR JAGR

POSITION:
Right Wing
TEAM:
Pittsburgh Penguins
SIGNED TO THE NHL:
1990

Career Facts:

- Jaromir has scored ninety points in a season seven times.
- Jaromir is one of the few players who has won the Stanley Cup and an Olympic gold medal.
- Jaromir was the youngest player to score three goals in an NHL game.
- The Penguin organization paid Jaromir $10.4 million to play the 1999-2000 season.

#10 PAVEL BURE

POSITION:
Right Wing
TEAMS:
Vancouver Canucks,
Florida Panthers
SIGNED TO THE NHL:
1991

Career Facts:

- Pavel has scored more than fifty goals in a season four times. He has reached sixty goals twice.
- Pavel was born in Russia. He is called the "Russian Rocket" because he skates so fast.
- Vancouver hockey fans voted Pavel the most exciting Canuck for four straight years.
- Pavel holds several records including the most points in a season by a Canuck.

#9 PAUL KARIYA

POSITION:
Left Wing
TEAM:
Anaheim Mighty
Ducks
SIGNED TO THE NHL:
1994

Career Fact:

- Paul was a runner-up for the Calder Trophy, which is given to the league's best rookie.
- In 1997, Paul finished second for the Hart Trophy. This is given to the league's Most Valuable Player (MVP).
- Paul has scored more than one hundred points in a season twice in his career.
- Paul wears the captain's "C" on his jersey.

#39 DOMINIK HASEK

POSITION:
Goaltender
TEAM:
Buffalo Sabres
SIGNED TO THE NHL:
1990

Career Facts:

- Dominik has one of the best records of any goaltender on the ice.
- For six straight years, Dominik led the league with the best **save** percentage.
- Dominik has won five Vezina trophies for being the league's top goalie.
- In 1998, Dominik won the Hart Trophy as the league's MVP. He is the only goaltender to ever win that award twice.

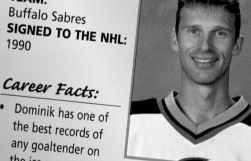
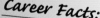

CHECK IT OUT

Keep track of your favorite hockey heroes at

www.allstarsites.com/links/ Hockey/NHL

Staying Healthy

Hockey players need to eat right so they can play hard. That starts with daily servings from all the food groups, including breads and cereals, fruits and vegetables, meats and proteins, and milk and milk products.

It is important for athletes to take in enough **calories**. Athletes, including hockey players, use up a lot more energy than people who do not exercise as much. Athletes need to choose the foods they eat wisely. Food can affect the way athletes perform.

Water is also very important. The body should always be properly **hydrated**. Sports drinks help to get liquids into the body quickly during practises and games. Players should also drink plenty of water every day, both while exercising and while resting.

Pasta is an excellent source of carbohydrates. Fruit also provides nutrients the body needs to keep healthy and active.

Most hockey players are extremely good athletes. Their muscles are strong, and athletes can exercise hard for long periods of time. To avoid injuries, they stretch their muscles well before and after a game or practise.

Players must be able to skate at full speed for quick bursts, and they must be able to play an entire game. That means hockey players need two different types of training: one to make them fast and another to build their **endurance**.

Bicycling and long-distance running are two activities athletes can perform to build up their endurance. Sprinting is a good way to build up speed. Hockey players often train with in-line skates, or roller blades. This keeps them in shape over the summer and makes them stronger skaters.

CHECK IT OUT

Learn more about eating healthy by visiting

www.dole5aday.com/menu/ kids/menu.htm

Hockey Brain Teasers

Test your knowledge of this exciting sport by trying to answer these hockey brain teasers!

Q How did hockey get its name?

A The word "hockey" probably comes from the French word "hoquet," which is a shepherd's crook. It refers to the tools used by Native peoples in early hockey games. It may also come from the Miqmac word "hoghee."

Q Can the puck be kicked into the net for a goal?

A No, the puck cannot be intentionally kicked in to score. A puck can be deflected, or knocked, off another player's body and go in for a goal.

Q How thick is the ice?

A The ice surface is best when it is three-quarters of an inch thick. If it is thicker, the layers become softer and "slower" to skate on.

Q How do players on the bench know when to change lines and what positions to play?

A All the players have set positions. Before the game, a coach may group players together into "lines." When one line gets tired and comes to the bench, the next line goes onto the ice.

Q When is a shot considered a goal?

A The puck must completely cross the goal line between the posts of the goalie net to be counted as a goal.

Q Why do goaltenders come out of their net during play?

A Goaltenders come out in front of the net to reduce the shooting area. They cut down the angle of the shooter or force the shooter to release a shot too wide.

Glossary

blade: the thin, flat part of a stick

boards: the barrier around a rink that keeps the puck and players inside

calories: energy values of food

draft: process used to select players for sports teams; the team that finishes in last place chooses first in the draft

endurance: the ability to continue an activity for a long time

enforce: to make sure rules are followed

face-off: when the referee drops the puck between two players

goal: when the whole puck crosses the red goal line and goes in the net

high-sticking: holding the blade of the hockey stick above shoulder level

hydrated: combined with water

mesh: an arrangement of interlocking links that form a net

offside: being beyond an allowed area or line before the puck

penalty: when a player breaks a rule; that player goes to the penalty box, and the team plays with fewer players

save: when a goaltender blocks a shot that would have been a goal

season: the length of time between opening day and the last playoff game. The professional hockey season begins in October and ends in June.

shifts: groups of players who play together for a set period of time and then come off the ice; another shift of players takes their place

Index